Android App Development Essentials

The Basics to Publishing a Successful App

By Raj Patel

Table of Contents

Introduction

This e-book is written for the complete beginner whose goal is to earn passive income through the development of Android applications. It would not be an understatement to claim that anyone with the right mentality can profit from Android apps. The best part is that aside from the one-time $25 developer fee for having a Google Play Developer Console account, it does not necessarily take money to make money. In this e-book, I guide you through everything from coming up with a successful app idea to publishing and marketing your application. You do not need any experience with Java programming or XML knowledge to earn passive income from Android applications. All that is required is persistency, the determination to make it happen, and your time.

It is easy to see where the money earning potential comes from; the more applications you have published, the more streams of passive income you have – and why limit yourself to Android? After learning the ins and outs of Android application development and publication, it would be strategic to expand to the iOS App Store and perhaps even the Windows Store. It is no surprise that some developers have even quit their day jobs and instead make their living off mobile applications. Success is all about choosing the right niche, creating a quality app, handling reviews, and most importantly, tactical monetization, all of which will be extensively covered throughout the chapters.

Fortunately, mobile apps allow anyone to reach a global audience. The number of people you can potentially reach upon releasing an Android app is almost limitless. You do not have to pay a single cent for advertising to extend your influence to literally thousands of users with your Android app. That is rather encouraging, as this type of reach did not exist in the past. Such an access to an immense user base can easily translate to significant earnings with the correct factors in place. Clearly the potential for great income exists, but these qualities must be strategically implemented. Discussion of these factors will be expounded upon in the upcoming chapter: **Qualities of a Successful App**.

The era of mobile applications is now; this is your opportunity to partake of the mobile app market and yield generous returns on your work. What is most attractive about this method of passive income is the low barrier of entry. No matter how knowledgeable you are with Android, you will have no trouble entering the mobile app market. I can attest from firsthand experience that even the most inexperienced newcomer can be successful in this endeavor. If you are truly determined to make passive income with Android a reality, you have chosen the correct book. Invest your time and effort in this avenue of income, and by following the guidelines illustrated in this Book, you will ultimately be rewarded in the end.

Regarding the apps you produce, it is imperative to maintain a quality over quantity ethic. Perhaps it is tempting for some to create a number of low quality apps in an attempt to milk as much money out of the users as possible, but this will not serve you well in in the end. Your apps would receive negative reviews and in the worst case scenario, your developer account could get banned depending on the circumstances, e.g., spam. The most compelling incentive for creating a quality app is that your app will rank higher, which converts to higher earnings. Develop with the users' best interests in mind and you are far more likely to be successful in the long run.

Qualities of a Successful App

Before we can begin brainstorming ideas for an application, it would be beneficial to recognize the factors of a successful app. This chapter highlights some prominent qualities of the most successful apps in the mobile app market. It is no secret that the odds are stacked against the common developer in one of their apps being a hit. There is no magic recipe that can guarantee your app will be successful, but there are certain factors that decide which apps will see success and which will ultimately fail. Some important key points to keep in mind are that the app must have a purpose and either entertain/educate, save time/money, or provide a useful service. Fundamentally, the goal is to create an app that people want, is easily discoverable, and provides benefits to the user.

Offer it for Free

For most users, free is the magic word in significantly increasing the odds of them downloading the app. Take a look at the top grossing apps in the Google Play Store. Interestingly enough, the vast majority of the top grossing apps are offered for free – and for good reason. Simply a price tag is enough to drive off potential app users. Couple this with the fact that paid applications are not available in all countries and the benefits of making it free become more apparent. Given this, it can safely be concluded that monetization is generally much more effective by making the app free and including ads with in-app purchases. It is worth mentioning that once you have established your app as free, you are not permitted to upgrade it to a paid one. Therefore, your monetization strategies should be planned out. Such strategies will be discussed in the **Monetization Tactics** chapter.

Shareability

Successful apps have historically integrated the ability to share the app via social networking. If people enjoy an app, they will likely tell others about it. Often times an incentive will be offered for sharing the app – this is quite the strategic method for encouraging your users to share the app. Designing the app to be easily shareable and offering some sort of in app reward for doing so is a surefire method of having your app gain additional exposure. As a general rule of thumb, apps that are easy to share will perform far better on average. With this feature in place, your app is basically automating the advertising for itself!

Retain Simplicity

Simplicity is easily a factor that contributes to the app's success, as it has been historically proven that it does not require complexity for an app to be successful. Simplicity is the key and is an often overlooked factor when aspiring developers attempt their first app. A confusing and complex user interface that makes it difficult for the user to navigate the app will only end up frustrating your customers and result in uninstalls. Apps only have one chance to impress the user, so it is important to keep in mind that a simple and appealing user interface is essential. If your app provides the same functions as another app, but is simpler to use and more visually appealing, consumers will generally choose your app instead. In order to corroborate the simplicity of your app, have your friends and family members test the prototype before releasing it. Any successful app can be simple, yet useful or captivating in some sort.

Handle Negative Reviews

No matter how well constructed your app is, the reality is that negative feedback is inevitable. Reading up on negative reviews will offer insight on potential problems or bugs with your app. All too often, developers neglect their customers' experience and forget about the app. This is a grave mistake – as new users would continue to complain with your app problems unresolved, not to mention the low ratings your app would continue to receive. Instead, developers should aim to seek a better understanding of where they are coming from and strive to be on the same page as their unhappy customers. It is important to recognize all feedback, as an update to your app is an indication that you care about your customers and will abate some of the bad reviews.

Advertise the App

Perhaps your app is of high quality, original, and useful or entertaining, but this would not matter if nobody knew your app even existed! Ensure that you set aside the time and effort for app promotion, as it is essential that people know about your app in the first place. Unfortunately, you cannot just publish your app and simply hope that people happen to stumble across it. Granted, there is the small, offset chance that your app will be quite successful without any advertising whatsoever, but the chances of this dwindle without some form of advertisement. You must utilize multiple channels so that your app is exposed to as many people as possible. Contrary to what some might believe, it does not always require spending money to promote your app. This will be covered in the **Marketing the App** chapter.

Play Store Optimization

With competition continuing to grow, it is easy for your app to get lost in an ocean of other apps. In order to drastically improve your odds of success, it is important that you optimize your app for not only the Play Store's search engine, but your app's profile page. There are a few key qualities in optimizing the first impression your app receives. These include:

- **Name**
- **Icon**
- **Description**
- **Screenshots**

The **name** of your app is the core of the app's success. This is, without a doubt, the biggest driver of discoverability for any app. People will search for particular keywords for whatever it is they are looking for. For example, if one were in search of a task killer app, that person would likely search something along the lines of 'task killer.' A key optimization tool to remember is that the name of your app should include the function of it as well – this will make it easier on users and significantly boost your app's discoverability. To summarize, name appeal is a huge driver of not only visibility, but app downloads.

An attractive **icon** makes a world of difference in whether users will even consider downloading the app. Assume your app easily shows up when users search for it. What good is this if users are uninterested and not even taking at a look at your app? Do not underestimate the importance of investing in your icon as it will pay dividends. Avoid word usage in the icon and keep its design consistent with the app design. Take a look at the top apps out there; their icons are simple and visually appealing. Contemporary android icon principles call for three dimensionality, a front view, and use of a distinct silhouette. First impressions count and an outstanding icon will undoubtedly result in driving more app downloads.

The first few lines of your app's **description** must be able to effectively convey its value to your prospective customers. Think of your app's profile as a sales page. You have just a few sentences above the expansion point to compel users to click to learn more about the app. Use attention grabbing information in the first few lines of your description that will pique your potential customers' curiosity and elicit them to read more about your app. This is your chance to finally convince consumers that your app is worth their time/money. You must be clear and concise in your description, otherwise a long-winded block of text will only serve to repel any potential users and result in a loss of downloads.

Customizing your **screenshots** is something that will be time well spent as they have a strong influence on users when downloading an app. A common mistake that app developers make is simply uploading their app's screenshots. Screenshots are eye catchers and people are generally more interested in pictures than descriptions. For this reason it is recommended to make your first screenshot as appealing as possible and unless your app is a game or rather simple, to use up all available screenshot slots. Your screenshots should reflect the functions of your app and why it is so great. Obviously, you cannot have good screenshots in the absence of an appealing design, which is something that should already be taken care of beforehand.

When you really invest the time and effort in providing the best possible presentation for your app, your app will stand out and users will notice. As you can see, Play Store optimization is quite the important tool in app discoverability and downloads. Following these general guidelines will ensure that your app stands out from the rest.

Application Ideas

You want to develop for Android, but your mind is a blank slate when it comes to development ideas. This scenario happens all too often and is a common problem for developers, especially for those that seek to publish multiple apps. Sometimes, it is not the programming that is the difficulty, but coming up with a successful app idea. On the other hand, some developers are seemingly able to release app after app. Unfortunately, there is no secret formula for brainstorming app ideas. However, this chapter encompasses some of the most useful methods for breaking the creativity barrier and figuring out what kind of app you want to develop.

Use Your Interests

What excites you? Do you have a passion for gaming? Perhaps movies are more your speed? Whatever your interests are, try discovering ways to implement that passion in the form of an app. Things that you enjoy can transition to wonderful topics for an app. Put that accumulated knowledge and wisdom to use in the form of a service oriented app. This could be anything ranging from written instructions to how to videos. As a general rule of thumb, try to include information in the app that you wish you knew when you first became immersed in whatever hobby or interest.

Analyze the Market

Take a look at the top charts for free and paid apps to see what is popular right now. Ask yourself this: why are these apps so popular and how did they get to the top of the charts? This is imperative because the top charts are basically cheat sheets into the minds of the common consumer. You need not reinvent the wheel; try to think about what you would do differently and how you could improve upon it. For every action or feature you access, you must ask yourself if there is an easier way to do it. The viewing of other apps has the potential to provoke an idea for an app of your own.

Fulfill a Need

If someone has a need for something, it is likely that others will have a need for that as well. The best ideas for apps stem from a real, personal need for them. Formerly needed apps would include flashlight apps, music recognition apps, and even things as simple as compass apps. Creating an app that fills a need means you must know your target audience and the type of information they are looking for. A great method of finding a need to fulfill is by asking your friends for ideas, or having them tell you of any function or problem that they have not yet fulfilled by an app. Better yet, try thinking of some of your problems that could be solved with an app.

Target a Specific Niche

Considering the immense size of the mobile app market, you would not want to spend a long time developing an app, only to find that duplicate apps already exist. Do not try to think of a product for everybody; instead try targeting a demographic or a specific niche of considerable size. After that, you can target interrelated niches and augment from there. Sure, you will not make as much money as an app that has mass appeal, but it will be much easier to make money, much less expensive, and your chances of success increase dramatically. However, you do not want your niche to be too obscure, or the app will obviously not sell well. This is the tricky part – finding the happy medium where the niche is not too small, but just large enough to have enough demand for the app.

Time Killer

Try thinking of the most popular games in the mobile app market as of now. A key factor in a time killing app is that it is easy for people to jump in and out of the app at their convenience. The successful, time filling apps have that special "it" factor which compels the user to repeatedly play the game. Due to its addictive nature, this also gives them another reason to tell others about your creation. Flashback to all the old video games, arcade games, board games, and other retro games that you had played back in the day. All that is required is a new twist on an old concept and you now have your app idea.

Select a Category

A strategic method of choosing your category is by noticing what type of applications you predominately have yourself. Perhaps you favor apps that are productive, or maybe you are the gamer type. If you have a diverse mixture of app categories and are having a difficult time choosing your favorite category, start searching the many different app categories in Google Play. Try imagining the different apps you could develop for each category. When you have selected your favorite category, you should search the apps under the said category. View the apps that grab your attention and download some of the free apps. It would be wise to familiarize yourself with everything there is to know about your category. By doing so, you are slowly, subconsciously formulating some ideas for an app.

Search the User Forums

User forums are a great channel for discovering an app idea that you could potentially pursue and develop. Simply search the various phone handset and development forums out there to get an idea of the apps that users are really looking for. Unique, simple app ideas are generally hard to come by, but occasionally you will find somebody in a forum who posts wishing that an app performed a certain function. It is likely you will even come across threads of users asking others for app development ideas. Just make sure that somebody else has not already developed the app and published it already. This falls under fulfilling a need and remember: if someone has a need for something, it is likely others will too.

Simply Browse the Market

If you are still having trouble formulating ideas for an app, why not simply browse the Play Store to see what is already out there? Once again, the observation of others' apps can potentially stimulate an idea for an app of your own. With so many great developers out there, this translates to great apps and ideas on the store. Be wary, however, that there are also many low quality apps out there that are either badly executed or just plain useless – these should clearly be avoided. Take a look at what stands out to you, download these apps, and have a play with them. Take notes on what you like about the app and what you do not like. You need not wait for the optimum idea for an app to come to mind, or you might never get started. Follow these rules, pick something, and just go for it!

Development Tools

This chapter describes the installation of the Java software required to run Eclipse and downloading the Android developer tools (ADT) necessary to develop Android apps. Eclipse is the leading, integrated development environment (IDE) used by professional programmers. Some of the more prominent tools in the ADT Bundle are listed and defined. This portion of the book is solely intended to aid aspiring Android app developers that wish to utilize Eclipse and program in Java in acquiring the necessary software and tools to do so. Experienced programmers and those in pursuit of alternatives to programming in Java can feel free to skip this chapter.

Download the Java SE Development Kit (JDK)

Before we can install Eclipse and its Android tools, we need to be certain that the proper Java software has been installed to enable Eclipse to run. It is recommended to install the newest version of Java to ensure that Eclipse will run. Download the latest version of the Java SE (Standard Edition) Development Kit from the oracle website. Accept the license agreement and choose the appropriate platform. Run the exe and choose your installation location. The Java Runtime Environment will also be installed with the JDK. Mac users can skip this step as the Mac OS X operating system already integrates the JDK.

Note: In case you are wondering and having difficulty choosing the appropriate JDK, x86 and x64 refers to a 32 and 64 bit operating system, respectively.

Set the Path Environment Variable

After you have installed the JDK, it is necessary to define your JDK path. This must be done or Eclipse will not run. Go to the "bin" folder found in the JDK folder and copy the link location. Next, go to "Edit Environmental Variables" found in the control panel under the category of system and security, system, and in advanced system settings. Click the advanced tab, then environment variables. Under user variables, click "Path" and edit. Do not delete any existing content, simply go to the end of the line and separate it with a semicolon – then you can paste the link of the bin. Click OK and you have successfully defined your JDK path.

Download the Android SDK

One of the very first steps is to download the Android SDK (software development kit) from the Android developer website itself. The ADT Bundle contains everything required in terms of Android tools to begin developing apps. The download includes, but is not limited to:

- **Eclipse + ADT plugin** (if you downloaded Eclipse separately, you would have to install the ADT plugin manually)
- **Android Tools** – these are the tools that help you develop apps for the Android platform, classified into two groups:

- o **Android SDK Tools** – this provides you with the API (application programming interface) libraries and developer tools necessary to quickly start developing apps. Ensure that you keep this up to date. Some prominent SDK tools include:
    - **Android SDK Manager** – this allows you to download and update the necessary tools, platforms, and other components
    - **AVD Manager** – this provides the graphical user interface to create and manager Android Virtual Devices (AVDs)
    - **Android Emulator** – as you may have inferred, this prototypes Android applications on a virtual mobile device emulator, which allows you to forego the need for an Android device
    - **Dalvik Debug Monitor Server** – this is a debugging tool which allows developers to discover and expunge bugs in apps running on either an emulator or physical Android device
  - o **Android Platform-tools** – these are customized to support the features of the latest Android platform and are typically updated upon installing a new SDK platform
- **The latest Android platform** – for every Android version there is one SDK platform, which includes an android.jar file. When developing, you must specify an SDK platform as your build target to build an Android app.
- **System images** – this is what the Android emulator requires to run

A word of caution: Do not move any of the folders or files in the bundle – moving the eclipse or SDK directory will result in ADT being unable to locate the SDK and you will have to manually update the ADT preferences. Of course, the ADT Bundle contains a vast array of many other SDK tools, but the aforementioned list outlines the basics.

Review

To summarize, here are the steps necessary to get started using Eclipse:

1. Download the latest version of the JDK from the <u>oracle website</u>. After you choose your platform and download it, run the exe and choose your installation location.
2. Set the environment variable for the JDK path.
3. Download the <u>ADT Bundle</u> from the developer website.
4. After you have downloaded the ADT Bundle, unzip the package and store the resulting folders at the appropriate Android directory of your choosing.
5. You can now open the Eclipse IDE located in the /eclipse folder.

Troubleshooting

This section is comprised of two of the most common Eclipse errors that users may encounter in the beginning when running Eclipse for the first time.

PATH error

If you run Eclipse and come across something along the lines of this for an error:

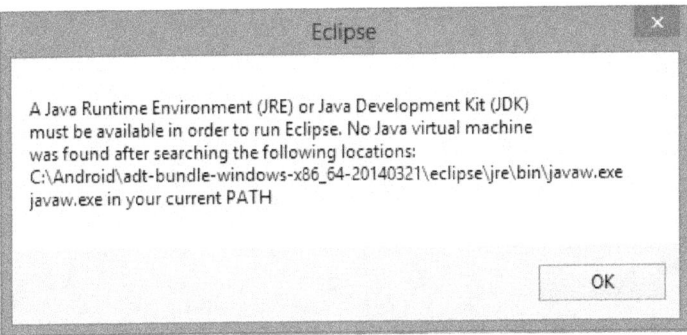

This means that you have not correctly defined your path environment variable. Ensure that you have installed the latest version of the JDK and that the path environment variable includes the Java installation's bin subdirectory.

JNI shared library error

This is another common error that users encounter when running Eclipse despite having their path environment variable set:

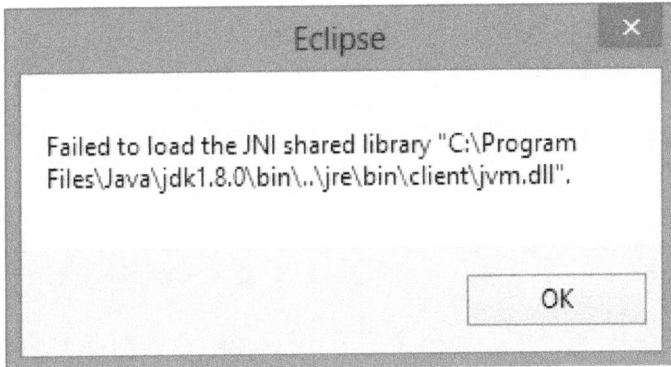

This means that your JDK and Eclipse program are not the same operating system. Both must be 32 bit or 64 bit. Once this has been rectified, Eclipse should be able to run.

Alternatives to Programming

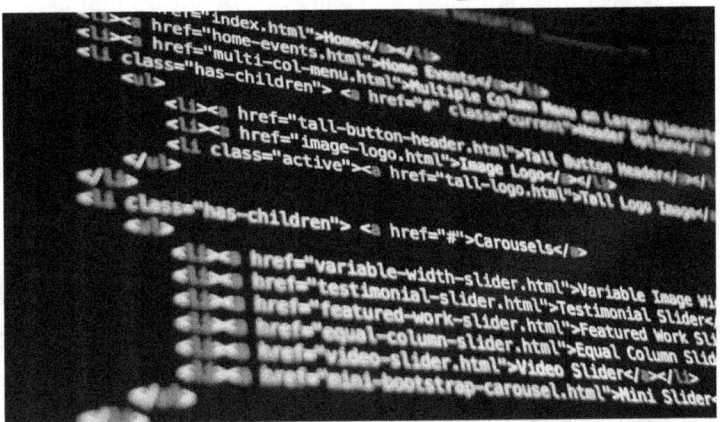

It is not about how the app was created. All that matters is the end product. Provided that the app is high quality and optimized for the Play Store, there is no reason how the app was developed will have an impact on success. You would be surprised at the successful apps out there that did not have to be programmed by the developer, but instead created with an alternative program. Regardless of how they were created, some of the most successful apps out there are not demanding in terms of coding. If you have aspired to publish your very own mobile application, but have feared the conventional route of programming with Eclipse, this chapter is for you. You can rest assured that none of that will be necessary, as this section of the book explores alternatives to learning how to program in Java and using Eclipse.

Use an Alternative Program

If you simply Google something along the lines of "how to create an app without coding", you will come across a list of results of app creating programs that do not require you to write a single line of code. Software tools that proclaim that anyone can create an app have been trending and emerging. Be wary of which tool you utilize to create your app, however, as some may severely limit you by what you can do with it. If your app idea is rather complex, you will need to ensure that you choose your software tool wisely. You would not want to begin working on an app, only to find out midway through that the program will not allow you to implement a certain feature. Starting all over again from scratch on a new software tool does not sound too appealing, so this is why it would be most beneficial to first play with the program and ensure that it is capable of meeting your demands. One should also be leery of software tools that charge a monthly fee to publish your application, as there are plenty of other tools that do not charge you on a recurring basis. Select your mobile app developing tool carefully, learn how to really utilize the program, and you will have no problem making your app idea a reality.

Find a Partner

In your mind, everything is set in stone – from the idea, design, functions, etc. For whatever reason, you are not interested in having to toil with the development process. If you do not mind giving up equity and control of your vision, find a developer who you can trust will not walk out mid-project and will look out for your best interests. You may be wondering what the difference is between partnering up with someone and outsourcing a developer. There are pros and cons to both options. While outsourcing would be paying a developer to code the app *for* you, partnering is working *with* someone to get the app published by any means necessary and sharing equity with that person. Because you are working with someone, your partner is likely to give his best effort. Partnering will also keep the costs low since you are sharing equity with someone – this is ideal for those who have limited funds.

Outsource a Freelancer

Unless you can afford to do so, this option should typically be treated as a last resort for those with limited funds. Should you choose to hire a freelancer to develop your app, you will have to either take care of support tickets, or hire someone to do that for you. You will also have to dispose more money on either the same or a different freelancer if you wish to update your app in the future. It is recommended that you hire a developer whose skills are ideal for your app idea. There are many freelance websites out there, so your options in choosing your developer are copious. Before you contact a freelance developer, ensure that you have a clear idea of what you want your app to do and have all the technicalities ironed out. Of course, you should check their credibility before contacting them to see if they are right for your product.

Hire a Development Shop

Hiring a development shop is a big decision and is not to be taken lightly; this is a viable alternative to outsourcing a freelancer if your app idea is quite complicated. A development shop is comprised by a team of people that generally consists of designers and developers. If you have the funds and are truly serious about making your app idea a reality, this may be the financial investment for you. Not only would it cost in excess of thousands of dollars, but you are going to invest a lot of time as well collaborating with the development shop about your app idea. Before you think of hiring a development shop, take the initiative to create an in depth blueprint of your idea and realistically stick to your scope of the product. Choosing the correct development shop can be a tricky business, as many development agencies differ in many aspects that you should look into. These include:

- **Price**

- **Domain Knowledge**
- **Team**
- **Design Capabilities**
- **Process**

The **price** is going to greatly vary among the many mobile development shops. Your app is likely going to cost in excess of thousands of dollars with a development agency, but when looking at a shop, you need to see if their estimates are reasonably within your budget. This is the first attribute that you must considering when choosing a shop; if the shop's price estimates are well above what you can afford to spend, that shop is not going to be a good fit.

The agency's **domain knowledge** should be highly pertinent to the type of app you want developed, especially if the field is rather complex. If your app idea is in a specialized field, this is most certainly an aspect you will want to consider. Choosing a firm with the appropriate domain knowledge will be most conducive towards your project. Such a firm will not only have the expertise built in and save time, but ultimately result in a higher quality app.

Knowing exactly what kind of **team** you are dealing with prior to hiring the shop would be rather beneficial. Find out what kind of resources the development agency provides and the average experience of their engineers. An even more pertinent matter is if the firm has a specified product manager who manages the entire process. Having an app built for Android means that you obviously want your development shop to be especially skilled and experienced with Android app development.

The **design capabilities** of the development team should be taken into account. Some agencies are more code oriented and keep the design relatively simple, while others employ adept graphic designers – making for high quality user interfaces. What type of experience would you prefer for your app, or perhaps you would rather opt for a hybrid? This is another reason why it is important to know what the firm's team is comprised of.

 Understanding the **process** of the development team is vital in being a proactive, active participant of the development process. Doing so is the difference between spending more money for additional, unplanned time and finishing the app before the deadline. Knowing if and when you can have in person meetings with your team would be important to collaborate and offer feedback. You will want to find out how often you will get status updates, along with how frequently you will receive a prototype of the app to test on your phone. Familiarizing yourself with the firm's process will allow you to actively participate with the development process, which will ensure that you do not end up under budget, but with a successfully completed app.

Obtaining Media

You are likely going to need images and perhaps sound effects or music for your app. You have probably figured out fairly quickly that you cannot just slap your favorite soundtrack or others' images on a project without infringing on copyrights. Doing so would result in a separate case of infringement for every download your app gets. Royalty free media is extremely important for first time developers – developers can use it without having to pay anyone. Royalty free media is any image or sound that you have the right to use free of royalty charges; however, there may be a one-time license fee to obtain the media. In the majority of cases, if the content is free, you will have to attribute credit to the original publisher. Conversely, most royalty free media that is paid for do not stipulate some kind of credit. Be warned, however, that not all stock media is permitted to be used for commercial purposes. Always ensure that you fully understand the restrictions on any royalty free music or stock photography that you want to use.

Types of Licenses

With many different licenses being used to supply stock media, it can be a little confusing to those unfamiliar with the industry. Some are very restrictive with usage, and some are actually quite lenient. Common licenses include:

- **Standard Royalty Free License**
- **Extended Royalty Free License**
- **Rights Managed License**
- **Creative Commons Licenses**
- **Public Domain**

The **Standard Royalty Free License** does not allow you to use the image or sound for unlimited use. There is a reproduction limit of the media which will vary depending on the source of the content. No one can predict the success of an app, but if it becomes a hit, the app's number of downloads could exceed the allowable copy limit. Free apps are allowed to utilize this type of license, but paid apps are not.

The **Extended Royalty Free License** is the highly preferred alternative to the standard version, as the permitted use is unlimited. You will want to stay on the side of caution; it is certainly worth the extra money to pay for this type of license as the mobile app market is unpredictable. Unlike the standard version, this license also allows for an image to be used in derivative products.

The **Rights Managed License** is not only very restrictive, but usually the most expensive method of purchasing stock media, as you pay to use their content on a per use basis. Many restrictions apply such as usage, size of image, placement, duration of use, and geographic distribution. You will have to submit information concerning intended use of the provided media, which ultimately determines yours rights granted. What is most beneficial about using this type of license, however, is that the purchase of the image or music under this license ensures that others cannot cash in using the same content. The products also tend to be higher quality under this license. This type of license weeds out inferior images as it eliminates the searching and sifting that is commonly experienced under royalty free media.

Creative Commons Licenses is a system of licenses created by a nonprofit organization that provides a range of creative works for others to legally use. Creative Commons licenses allow artists and photographers to protect their work while still providing their work free of charge to the public. Please keep in mind that an attribution to the original creator is always required with this type of license. There are six Creative Commons licenses and its terms and restrictions:

- **Attribution:** the most accommodating licenses of them all, this license allows you to copy, distribute, display, remix, and build upon their work
- **Attribution-No Derivatives:** you may copy, distribute, and display the work as long as the content is absolutely unchanged
- **Attribution-Non-Commercial-No Derivatives:** you may copy, distribute, and display the work as long as no changes have been made, but the work cannot be used commercially
- **Attribution-Non-Commercial:** this license allows you to copy, distribute, display, remix, and build upon their work, but only for non-commercial purposes
- **Attribution-Non-Commercial-Share Alike:** you may copy, distribute, display, remix, and build upon their work, but only for non-commercial purposes, and you must license your new creation(s) under the same license
- **Attribution-Share Alike:** you may copy, distribute, display, remix, and build upon their work, but you must license your new creation(s) under the same license

Public Domain offers the most unrestricted content you will find. There is no prior permission required, no attribution stipulated, and it is completely free. The creative materials are not protected in any shape or form by intellectual property laws that include copyright, trademark, or patent laws. As you can imagine, the quality and choice of content is rather limited. However, if you can find something worth using in your app, you should most certainly use it.

Royalty Free Music

Many of us either do not wish to spend money on a music composer, or cannot afford to do so. Combine this with the fact that you may not have a knack for creating music, and you may have had a problem were it not for royalty free music. What is most enticing about royalty free music is that even if your app is successful, you are not responsible for paying extra money. Clearly, this is a much better deal than trying to purchase the rights to use well known music that is not royalty free. If your app is a game and you want to implement an instrumental track, then it would be worthwhile to take your time in choosing an appropriate track for your game. Choosing the right soundtrack can make all the difference in your success. Be aware, however, that digging through all the royalty free music you can find is a rather time consuming process – a stark contrast to the time you would spend going through stock free images because you have to listen to them one by one.

Free Stock Images

Similar to the previous case of audio, perhaps you are not interested in spending money on a designer or cannot afford one. Unless you are skilled in the verse of manipulating and creating images, you will probably need to resort to stock photography. This is generally the favored alternative to hiring a designer, as it will save time, effort, and money. As mentioned before, ensure that the image is permitted to be used for an unlimited number of times. You will occasionally have need of a graphical design for your app's background. It is also likely you will require icons to navigate your app, such as the settings icon for your user interface. Even if you do know your way around a graphics editing program, it is better if you do not spend excessive time and work into designing these graphical elements yourself. This is so your time can be invested on the most important functions and features of the app.

Monetization Tactics

This chapter delves into the reason why some people develop mobile applications in the first place: monetization. As the world is slowly becoming more driven and integrated with mobile applications, it has never been more important for developers to devise a successful monetization strategy. Developing a great app is one thing, but successfully monetizing it is another story. Executing monetization tactics strategically will secure you a return on your time and perhaps money spent on the app. Such a return can provide you with the funds necessary to finance even better apps in the future. In this chapter, you will find a number of commonly used monetization strategies and how they should be implemented into your apps. Despite the fierce competition, app monetization options have never been as prevalent as they are now. Successful app monetization is no easy feat, but by taking into account a multitude of factors and making informed decisions, you should be able to maximum the return from your app.

Paid Apps

This is the most basic, straightforward method of turning a profit from your app. You are guaranteed to earn money as users download the app, but on the other hand, the number of downloads your app receives significantly diminishes. Another downside is that because users are paying for your app, they will hold higher expectations for your app and have a lower tolerance for any bugs that may arise. Furthermore, paid apps are continuing to decline in popularity and are dominated by the freemium model. If you are still convinced in selecting premium by default, there are a couple strategies you can employ to maximize your return with this model. Ensure that you price the app no higher than 99 cents, as your app will enter the market at a disadvantage if you go above this price point. Secondly, unless your app provides a compelling reason to do so, most consumers are not going to be eager to purchase your app. If your app is under a special, niche category that makes life easier in some way or is truly high quality, then perhaps its usefulness warrants the premium.

In App Advertising

Advertising is not only the simplest method of monetizing a free app, but has historically been one of the most lucrative strategies as well. The overwhelmingly majority of users prefer a free version of an app with ads as opposed to having to pay for it. Ideally, a free version of your app with ads implemented would be published along with a paid version without the ads, as this is the most established structure. New developers will gain a love/hate relationship for advertising, enjoying the profits but hating the experience it creates for the user. It should be ensured that the ads placed do not negatively impact the user experience of the app, but instead naturally integrate with your app and feel less intrusive. One of the most effective, profitable ad placement strategies involves the positioning of interstitial ads between game levels or any natural breaks in the app. There are various advertising agencies you can sign up with, one of the most commonly used ones being Google AdMob. Of course, the rates of pay you earn from your app will be rather small and in order to generate significant income, your app will need to have considerable traffic. Obtaining traffic for your app will be included in the **Marketing the App** chapter.

In App Purchases

In app purchases are an excellent method of monetization, providing yet another opportunity for the developer to earn money even after the app has already been downloaded or purchased. Similar to advertising, this monetization strategy offers the best of both worlds by allowing the developer to offer the app for free and still monetize it with in app products and upgrades. Unlike advertisements, in app purchases are not generally viewed as annoying or intrusive to the user experience. Fortunately, there is minimum risk of in app purchases driving users away in annoyance. If you have an addicting game or an app that people like, it should not be too difficult to persuade some of your users to pay for the extra in app content. Naturally, when using the freemium model, you want as large a percentage of your free users as possible to purchase something. This is challenging, however, given that most users do not end up buying something in apps in general. Therefore, app developers should not shy away by attempting to incorporate in app purchases in subtle ways. Instead, let them be known and increase the temptation to purchase them by raising the incentives. Execute this monetization option strategically and your financial success with the app will most certainly improve.

Sponsorships

Sponsorships are a more involved sales process that would work well with apps that attract a niche group of people so that partners can have their brand sponsored to the appropriate audience. This is another effective tactic of generating an additional source of revenue without expending too many resources. An example of this monetization option would be placing the logo of a company somewhere on your app. The key is finding a sponsor that relates to the app's content so that the target audience of your app might be interested in it. This usually involves a partner that temporarily has ownership of your ad space. Of course, your app will need to be rather popular for this method, as you will need the contacts to access this monetization method. Sponsorships are similar to the ad supported model, only the ads are better targeted. You also have better control over the type of ads, size, placement, and even its rate of occurrence. As a result, sponsorships can be more thoughtfully integrated into the app. Because the ads target the audience very well, they seem less invasive than completely random ones. This often translates to higher earnings from the users clicking the ads more frequently since the content is actually related to the app.

Publishing to Play Store

Using whatever method you chose in order to develop your app, you now have the APK file and are completely finished with monetization methods in place or planned ahead. You may be wondering how you can get started with distributing your app to the public. As mentioned in the first chapter, you will need to pay a one-time $25 developer fee for registering a Google play developer account. However, this should be nothing more than a negligible expense considering the limitless potential for financial gain in the mobile app market. Just as a reminder, you must decide whether or not you want to charge money for your application before publishing. You can transition your paid app to free, but cannot revert a free app back to paid. Once the app is free, it will always be free. Also keep this in mind: Should you choose to sell the app, include in app purchases, or offer subscriptions, you will also need to set up a Google Wallet Merchant account. The following in this chapter will expedite the process of publishing your app and make it seamless.

Register a Google Play Developer Account

This is the first and simplest step towards publishing your app in the Google Play Store. Search the Google Play Developer Console or navigate here and sign in with your Google account. If you do not already have a Google account, you will need to register one before signing up for the developer account. Agree to the Google Play Developer distribution agreement and continue to pay the $25 payment. You will be notified of your verification via email. It is now possible to publish applications on Google Play!

Register a Google Wallet Merchant Account

If you do not plan on making your apps paid, selling in app purchases, or offering subscriptions, you can skip this. Otherwise, you will need to register and link a Google Wallet Merchant account. After logging in to your Google Play Developer Console, click on "Financial Reports" and you can set up the merchant account from there. It is important to note that once you link a wallet merchant account to your developer account, they cannot be unlinked for any reason.

Promotional Assets

There are several features that you will need to have prepared before you can publish your app. The use of high quality media to illustrate the features and functionality of your app is essential in attracting new users. You will obviously need the APK file of the app, but these are the promotional assets that are required:

- **Application Icon**
- **High Resolution Launcher Icon**
- **Screenshots**

Your **application icon** should be optimized to support the various screen densities. Screen resolutions can range from a small device to a large, almost two handed sized device. This is why it is important to design your icon in multiple sizes. All Android phones can be classified by 5 primary screen densities, which are medium (MDPI), high (HDPI), x-high (XHDPI), xx-high (XXHDPI), and xxx-high (XXXHDPI). Google recommends following the 2:3:4:6:8 ratio between these 5 densities, respectively. The baseline asset, which is the medium density asset, is 48x48 pixels. It should be noted that the dots per inch (dpi) are a measurement of screen density; the higher the dpi, the higher the screen density and the more detail that can be shown in an image. Below is a table to give a better idea of the required resolutions:

1x MDPI ~160 dpi	1.5x HDPI ~240 dpi	2x XHDPI ~320 dpi	3x XXHDPI ~480 dpi	4x XXXHDPI ~640 dpi
48 x 48 px	72 x 72 px	96 x 96 px	144 x 144 px	192 x 192 px

By offering your application icon in multiple sizes to support the above resolutions, your icon will appear high quality on all devices.

A **high resolution launcher icon** is required and used in various locations on Google Play. Its dimensions are to be 512px by 512px, a 32-bit PNG with an alpha channel, and have a maximum file size of 1024 kilobytes. Although the high resolution icon does not replace the app's launcher icon, it should be a higher resolution version of it.

A minimum of 2 **screenshots** are to be uploaded, with a maximum of 8 being allowed. The minimum dimension of your screenshots can be 320px and the maximum is 3840px. Your maximum dimension cannot exceed twice the length of your minimum dimension. The dimensions are recommended to be 320w x 480h, 480w x 800h, or 480w x 854h. The image format is required to be either JPEG or 24-bit PNG without an alpha channel.

Some optional features include:

- **Promotional Graphic**
- **Feature Graphic**
- **Promotional Text**
- **Promotional Video**

The **promotional graphic** is used only for promotions of your app on versions of the Android OS earlier than 4.0 and is optional. If you wish to cater to users of older android devices and versions, the dimensions are to be 180px by 120px and the image format should be either JPEG or 24-bit PNG with no alpha channel.

The **feature graphic**, although optional, is something that you should definitely consider uploading because it is required in order to be featured anywhere on Google Play. The image format is JPEG or 24-bit PNG with no alpha channel and the dimensions are 1024px by 500px. Google recommends using a safe frame of 924x400 with 50px of safe padding on each side, which means that all of the important content should be within this safe frame.

The **promotional text** is the text that would accompany your feature graphic if your app happened to be featured on Google Play. This should be written, as you never know if your app could be featured on the Play Store.

A **promotional video** entails adding the URL to a YouTube video to demonstrate the application and should be kept short at 30 seconds to 2 minutes, focusing on the best parts about your app. While it may not be the driving force of downloads, it will certainly result in increased brand awareness.

Publishing the App

At this point, the promotional assets that are required to publish your app should be prepared so that you can upload the application to

Google Play. Since you have had the materials prepared beforehand, publishing should now be a fairly straightforward process. Here are the steps to publish your app:

1. Login to the Google Play Developer Console.
2. Click "Add new application".
3. Enter the title and choose to upload the APK first.
4. Complete the store listing using the promotional assets you prepared.
5. In the Pricing & Distribution section, select whether your app is free or paid and the countries you will distribute the app to.
6. If you have any app in products, do not forget to include this in the In-App Products section.
7. After completing all the necessary fields, you can now publish your application to Google Play!

Marketing the App

As the perpetually expanding mobile app market continues to augment, it can be rather difficult at times for app developers to differentiate their products. Would it not be infuriating and discouraging to spend weeks or even months developing an app that hardly anyone downloads or purchases? This is a scary possibility, so do not let this happen to you. Unfortunately, it is not good enough to simply publish a great app and wait for the money to roll in. Many factors that should already be in place have been discussed, such as creating a stunning icon, writing a captivating description, and using a great title for the app. After publishing, however, there are still many methods of promotion you can employ to secure maximum exposure. Now that your app is live, it is your responsibility to push awareness of your product and to ensure that your target audience knows about it. Contrary to popular belief, it is not always required to spend money on advertising, as many app entrepreneurs became successful promoting their apps for free. In this chapter, you will discover numerous, free/cheap methods of advertising your app.

Utilize Social Media

It is highly recommended to reach out to as many channels of social networks as you can. Regardless of financial resources or popularity, social media gives the opportunity to gradually build an audience over time. This can be accomplished by offering great content that promotes your app, such as writing a blog post about your app, creating a video showcasing its main features, and sharing it via social networking. Once your popularity starts gaining momentum, you will want to ensure that you continue to keep people engaged with such content more than ever and to maintain a long term commitment to your community. While social media is certainly not something that you can put on autopilot, you can passively increase your fan-base by offering in app incentives to users for sharing your app via social networking.

Create a Microsite for Your App

Take cues from the most successful apps out there; most, if not all of the top apps have a microsite promoting their app and possibly other apps as well. Your app will fare better in terms of exposure and downloads with the creation of a microsite. Microsites offer a convenient location for redirecting prospective consumers to find out more about your app. Just as you would on the Play Store, you can share everything about the app that ranges from screenshots, videos, and text. You can also offer the link(s) to download the app as well as contact information. The complexity of the site can range from one simple page to several pages, depending on how intricate your app is. Your microsite can also serve as an all-purpose site to promote all of your apps instead, or you could ideally have both a microsite for one app and another for all of your apps.

Pitch your App to the Media

Every app developer wants his app to be reviewed by a well-established person or website, as the boost in awareness and installs are quite significant. Unless your app is mediocre, there is no reason you should not reach out to journalists, reporters, and well known bloggers to evaluate your product. Ensure that whomever you contact has some degree of relevance to your app; for example, a person that reviews iPhone games will probably not want to review your productivity Android app. While this is a great method for pushing awareness, these types of people receive countless pitches from other app developers alike. This is why it is important to differentiate your email from others and to make it appealing to the person you are contacting. When contacting a prominent reviewer via email, it is imperative that a few key features be included in your pitch:

- Title of the app
- Price
- Link to app
- Attached screenshots
- Description
- Video (if applicable)
- Contact information

With these main points addressed, your email will better stand out and it is more likely that the message will be responded to favorably.

Cross Promotion

The idea of cross promotion is to form a mutually beneficial partnership with another developer or company to promote each other's apps. This is a strategic partnership for new indie developers to pursue, but it must be ensured that the partner also has traffic, or the results will be fruitless. As you may have deduced, the concept is that you would be receiving as much traffic as you are giving to your partner. Advantages of this type of advertising entail a win-win situation for the partners, simultaneous promotion of each other, and the fact that it is an easy and often successful marketing strategy. What is great about this method of advertisement is that it is free and very low risk – even if your partner does not promote you while you promote them, you can easily rectify the situation by changing your ads. A similar, alternative method of cross promotion is if you have more than one app published, you can also use your own apps to cross promote your other apps.

Create a Video

Showcasing how great your app is in a video is an excellent method of spreading awareness of your app. Sometimes, screenshots do not properly capture the essence of your app, which is where a video comes in to play. Not only do consumers generally prefer visual content, but it is a more engaging method of presenting your app to prospective users. Videos are easy to share and thus have the potential to rapidly spread and become viral. These are some of the key points for optimizing your mobile app video and boosting visibility:

- Keep it short and concise at 30 seconds to 2 minutes
- Stay simple and reveal the best parts about the app
- Upload the video to as many video sites as you can
- Link your app's product page in your video descriptions
- If you have a microsite, embed the video there as well

Simply setup your camera and record yourself using the app. With some clever editing and by recording the best parts about the app, your teaser can end up looking quite professional.

Email Marketing

This is an often overlooked, but powerful marketing tool for reaching out to your audience and growing your customer base. By implementing this feature in your microsite, you can collect the email addresses of your users. If you have an app update, video, a new app, or any other content, you can let your audience know by sending an update to your email list. What is most enticing about this marketing method is that you have full control over your message and presentation. Growing your email list provides not only the opportunity to announce updates and keep in touch with subscribers, but to collect valuable feedback regarding your products. To reduce the burden of work, consider the use of autoresponders which send out emails to subscribers automatically when triggered by certain events, such as welcome emails.

Closing Words

Hopefully, you have learned something from this book that you can personally apply for yourself in the journey for passive income with Android. The market for mobile applications is definitely there; with billions of smartphones in the world outnumbering computers 5 to 1, smartphones have been overshadowing computers in sales since 2011. With such an immense mobile app market that continues to grow, it has never been more important to carefully optimize your app's features and promotion tactics. Remember that the most important step is getting started, whichever method you choose. Reading any random book is not going to guarantee you success in the mobile app market, but how you utilize the information that you acquire is what ultimately decides your fate. Applying the information in this book is bound to differentiate your app and help you obtain success.

If you have found my work to be useful, please feel free to leave a review.

www.ingramcontent.com/pod-product-compliance
Lightning Source LLC
Chambersburg PA
CBHW070337190526
45169CB00005B/1936